Jan's pancake

Story written by Cynthia Rider
Illustrated by Tim Archbold

C000051478

Speed Sounds

Consonants   *Ask children to say the sounds.*

f	l	m	n	r	s	v	z	sh	th	ng
ff	ll		nn		(ss)	(ve)	zz			nk
							s			

b	c	d	g	h	j	p	qu	t	w	x	y	ch
bb	k		gg					tt	(wh)			(tch)
	ck											

Each box contains one sound but sometimes more than one grapheme.
*Focus graphemes for this story are **circled**.*

Vowels

Ask children to say the sounds in and out of order.

a	e	i	o	u
at	hen	in	on	up

ay	ee	igh	ow	oo
day	see	high	blow	zoo

Story Green Words

Ask children to read the words first in Fred Talk and then say the word.

Jan   Dan   whisk   pop   pan   toss   flip   if
ran   pan   splat   hat

Ask children to read the root first and then the whole word with the ending.

let → let's

Red Words

said	the	you
for*	pancake*	do
your	be	he
my	of	I

* Red Word in this book only

Jan's pancake

Introduction

Do you like pancakes? Jan, the girl in the story, loves them. When she fancies making a pancake, her brother Dan helps her. Jan enjoys mixing up the pancake batter and then Dan cooks it.

Have you ever seen someone toss a pancake over to cook the other side? It's not easy – as Dan and Jan find out!

"Let's have a pancake," said Jan.

"Mix it, whisk it,
pop it in a pan,

toss it, flip it,
catch it if you can."

Up went the pancake.

"Catch it!" said Jan.

Dan ran with the pan.

Splat!

A pancake hat for Jan!

Questions to talk about

Ask children to TTYP for each question using 'Fastest finger' (FF) or 'Have a think' (HaT).

p.8　(FF)　What does Jan want to do?

p.9　(FF)　What does Jan do to make the pancake?

p.10　(FF)　What does Dan do to make the pancake?

p.13　(HaT)　Does Dan catch the pancake?

　　　(HaT)　How does Jan feel about what has happened?
　　　　　　(Look at the picture to help.)